Journey
INTO *Hope*

Journey

INTO Hope

Julie Clark

To order additional copies of this book, contact:
Xlibris Corporation
0-800-644-6988
www.xlibrispublishing.co.uk
Orders@xlibrispublishing.co.uk
302568

All poems are now in the data base. Praise God

CONTENTS

Acknowledgements..9

SECTION 1: Wordly Poems 13
Bedtime Again...14
The Wind In The Trees 15
My New Life 16
Panic Alert..17
The Walls Are Closing In 18
Who Will Stand Up 19
All I Want 20
Friends Are Important 21
What Do You Do 22
Your Love Is Like 23
A Babling Stream 24

Section 2: Questions 25
Oh My Child 26
Precious Things 27
Anouther Day In Paradise 28
The World Or Jesus...29
Lifes Challenges 30
Which Way 31

Section 3: Seeking and drawing...........................33
Back Into My Life 34
When You Feel You Can't Go On 35
Turn Again My Precious Child 36

The Ever Near Friend 37

Thoughts Of Jesus 38

Rest 39

Lift My Spirit 40

At The Foot Of The Cross 41

Father Please Take Me 42

Section 4: Heaven and earth respond 43

The Open Door 44

Sinner Come Back 45

Submit To Jesus 46

Thoughts Of Jesus 47

Kneel Before The Throne 48

Look At The Good 49

A Resonse From The Lord 50

Trust Me 51

A Woman Sits Alone And Crys 52

Gentle Spirit, Gentle God 53

Section 5: Challenging others 55

The Price Has Been Paid 56

When Churches Come Together 58

Gods Workers Are Few 59

The Man By The Sea 60

Look To The Cross 61

Christ And The Accuser 62

Does Anyone Know 64

Section 6: Blessings and gifts 65

Power Of The King 66

He Is My Lord 67

Your Throne Of Grace 68

Trust For The Future 70

Prophetic Poem 71
Kneel Before The Throne 72

Section 7: A walk of faith............................ 74

In The Stillness Of The Morning 74
Be Encouraged. 75
By His Stripes I Am Healed..76
Give Me A Servant Heart 77
Honor The Lord 78
Jesus My Lord 79
Go In Faith 80
With My Spirit..81

ACKNOWLEDGEMENTS

I would like to thank God for the opportunity

to share these poems with you. My wonderful husband Keith and sons Andrew and Matthew, for listening to my poems and helping to get them just the way they need to be and for putting up with the times I was not with them having my head stuck in the computer. For my mum and dad and family who have supported me over the years

Also Living Waters Fellowship in Manston Kent who have helped me by listening to the poems and giving me the confidence to use them in different ways

And finally Gerard Leo for the inside cover photo and the other photos he has shared with me that have inspired some of my later poems

My name is Julie Clark and I am from Kent UK

I am a born again Christian and I am married with two boys

I have been writing poetry since I was sixteen when I moved away from my parent's home to a live in job at a Christian conference centre

I was very nervous but made it through the first day, in the evening we went to a concert with Adrian Snell and one of the songs touched me, I went home and listened to it again and I felt peace, then I got two sentences in my mind and they kept rolling around, so I decide to write them down and that is when the rest of it came and my new poem was born and so was a gift that is precious to me and stayed with me for over 30 years

I won't say it has been an easy ride but I have always known the Love of Jesus in my life even when I walked away for a year he never left my side.

So I would like to share, with you the poems that the Lord has blessed me with, I pray that they will touch your hearts, and encourage you and maybe even challenge you, but my biggest prayer, and hope is that the Glory, Honor and Praise goes to my everlasting Savior Lord and King. This book is divided into seven sections and can be read as a journey to Jesus or just dipped into any time

Amen

SECTION I

Worldly poems

These poems were written about me growing up all about the feelings that I had when I was not yet a Christian and also when I wandered away from the lord for a year. It was a stressful time for me but God was always there for me

Bedtime Again

The light goes out and I'm alone
Well not really alone in my little room
As I lay on my back and drift to sleep
I listen to the wind in the trees
Rustling the leaves to and throe

The wind outside is strong today
But I don't mind I'm snug and warm
Down below are mum and dad
Talking, laughing, watching TV
Oh why is bed time such a drag

Now the house is quiet and still
Four feet are climbing up the stairs
The light in the hall goes off once more
I close my eyes up really tight
Lord bring me safe till morning light

The Wind In The Trees

The wind in the trees
Make you feel alive
It's quick and slow
As it comes and goes

The wind outside is strong today
And I did so much want to go and play
Out in the crisp fresh autumn air
Oh it really just isn't fair
Still it makes our windmill turn

Our windmill stands upon a hill
On a day like this it is never still
It turns the wheel that grinds the wheat
Makes us so many nice things to eat

The wind in the sail makes a lovely sound
As they go whirling around and around
There's good in everything we see
So that why we should always happy be

My New Life

My new life has started
In my small homely room
My heart gives a cheer
Now from the nest I have departed

A bed and a pillow to lay my head
Bright colored scatter cushions all around
Pictures are hanging upon the wall
My daddy's donkey the best of them all

My own little cooker, table and chairs
No longer food will I have to share
I can cook three meals square
Without a single worry or care

How long I have dreamed
Now its obvious plain to see
I've got my home, oh what joy
To know that is no longer just a dream

Panic Alert

Panic alert, panic alert
Got to get out, got to desert
All the old fears, all the old hurts
Nobody knows, nobody dares

You open the door, and you open your fear
Maybe I will leave it another day
For people outside, it's easy to say
Pull yourself together now on your way

Now at last you see the light
And life is not so much of a fight
But still for a while you will get a fright
And have to fight it with all your might

And now at last you can take up the cup
And all of the good things you can sup
You've pulled yourself through to something new
To open the door with confidence to know
That panic alert won't happen to you

The Walls Are Closing In

The walls are closing in on me
Closing, closing till I can not see
See the logic, see the sense
Why oh why do I feel so tense?

Shut in my room alone with my fear
Cried out for love special and true
Now I have found a love that is new
Genuine love that fresh every day

Someone he loves me, some one he cares
All my sorrows and fears to share
The love I have found will always be there
To help me put away my fears

Who Will Stand Up

Who will stand up for the children?
Where will they go when they feel the pain?
When they want to talk, but no one is listening
They don't understand or just don't care

Who will take time to talk to the children?
Who will take the time to listen and care?
Get involved if they dare
And most of all will they always be there

Who will support the vital work?
That people who care do each day
To them its not "just another child"
It's a child that needs patience and love

A difficult child needs patience and love
To find out where the real problem lies
To break the pain or physical ties
To release that child to a world full of hope

All I Want

All I want is a little respect
I am not stupid as you suspect
I don't need the whispers I don't need the stares
As if to say we really don't care

I am a normal human being
And all of my life I've hearing and seeing
Your reactions to the sight of my chair
And me the person it has to bare

I feel, I love the same as you
I need to be loved my someone too
So come and say "hi oh please please do"
Because I am only human too

Just because I have this chair
Still at night I cook my meals
I take the hand that my life may hold
So to this chair I put this seal

Of approval not of hate
And now at last I have found my Kate
I always knew it was never too late
For me a loving wife to take

So remember me when you see a chair
And take the time to really care
There is so much to give, so much to share
With a man in the corner in a wheel chair

Friends Are Important

Friends are important as you know
Friends to love and friends to care
Share those dreams that are deep
All your secrets forever to keep

A positive thought when you lay to sleep
Every thought for ever to keep
Every need they'll be happy to meet
And every problem so to beat

Dreams can come true if you have a friend
And will your broken heart to mend
Break all the barriers in your mind
And in you perfect happiness find

They give you all the time you need
And all your warnings you will heed
They'll give so freely without greed
And not a single thought of self.

What Do You Do

What do you do when you get board?
Do you turn to your fantasy or go for a walk
Do you think of the things you cannot afford?
Or go to the garden and pick up a fork

What do you do when it's pouring with rain?
And in your head you have a great pain
Do you give up again and go for a rest
Or do something that you enjoy the best

When you're feeling low and depressed
And for a party you feel poorly dressed
Think of all the good in your life
And that will put away all sighs of stress

So are you positive or negative today
Will you cry or smile come what may
If you feel happy you will have a good day
If you feel sad you'll just hide away

Your Love Is Like

Your love is like a shady oak tree
Sheltering a lamb from a cold north wind
Your love is like an apple tree
Quenching my thirst with the fruits of your love
Your love is like an April shower
Cooling me down when I get mad

Your love is like a sleeping child
At peace with the world outside
Your love is as sweet as sugar
Taking away all my bitter thoughts
Your love is like a flowing stream
Giving life where ever you go

Babling Stream

A babling stream, a peaceful lane
These are the things that I enjoy
As I walk on a summers day
With a warm gentle breeze upon my face

A cottage in a field, with swirling smoke
A family sitting round ready to eat
Rich chicken soup and freshly baked bread
Then five little children all snug in their bed

A flitting bird upon the nest
Protecting her brood from unknown harm
A cow chewing cud all gentle and calm
Then sheep and one dog in one accord

Oh what a beautiful land we have
If we would take the time to see
Instead of rushing through the day
Let's sit for a while and take it all in

SECTION 2

Questions

This is when I started to question what life was all about and wanted to make sense of the world and it tells how God finally started calling me to himself

Oh My Child

Oh my child small and young.
Going your own, sweet selfish way.
When will you learn to trust me more?
And learn to accept the things that I say?

Oh my child my dear sweet child.
I know deep longings in your heart.
But trust in me and you will see.
The best relationship to have is me.

So lay your heart down at the cross.
Learn to love and trust me more.
I will never leave you all alone.
So give up fighting and rest in me.

Precious Things

You may have a credit card.
And a mountain of debts and bills.
But does it make the flowers bloom.
And send the falling rain.

You may have all the gadgets.
That human money can buy.
But do they bring, love joy, and hope.
Rest and peace to a weary soul

You may have a big house.
And be the talk of the town.
But when the storms of life come round
Does it crumble at your feet?

You may be driving the biggest car.
That will take you near or far.
But does it straighten out the road.
And make your ways more clear.

There is a God who gives his grace.
No man made idol could take his place.
He made our hearts to live for him
Learn to trust and love him more

The greatest gift this Christmas
Is the savior of the world!
To lift our hands, in awe and praise.
To give our lives, to the maker of all.

Another Day In Paradise

Why do those people have no home?
Why isn't one bit of loving shown?
The pain they feel can never been shown
You're never around to hear them groan

Have a little patience show them that you care
How would you feel if you too was there
A big hole from just a tiny hole
Does no one have time Gods love to share?

So spare a thought for the lonely today
Spare a thought for those without a home
We have a home and someone to care

The simple things that we have
Is something they may never had?
They are not bad but isn't sad
So why not stop and make one glad

All they need is the loving touch
All they need is a kindly word
To all of us it doesn't take much
To them it's more than money can buy

The World Or Jesus

If I could give you the world I would.
But it wouldn't ease the pain.
If I could give you the world at peace I would.
But real peace comes from God alone.
If I could give you a large house I would.
But only my father can give this to you.

If I gave you a bible what would you do?
Would you read it or hide it away.
If I gave you my love what would you do?
Would you accept or turn in fear.
If I gave you God's peace what would you do?
Would you rest or still worry and fear.

Would you look to my Jesus?
Or look to the world.
Would you give him your life?
Or wander away.
Would you accept his love and words today?
Or would you just turn away.

The choice is yours I cannot say more.
Will you in faith fling open the door?
Or stay shut away in pride and fear.
Would you trust in my Jesus?
Or face him in death

Lifes Challenges

The ultimate test in this life today.
Is to put our trust in the unseen things.
Of God and his Spirit and the Son.
The trinity, the three in one.

What are the things that are truly unknown?
What are the things that are truly unseen?
We talk about Jesus and the unknown God.
We talk of the spirit and the unseen wind.

But take a look at the world out there.
And take the time; reach out and care.
We have a guide in this crazy world.
The ultimate we can do is care.

To touch a hand, to comfort a friend.
A prayer whispered low, to the father above.
Some bread for the table, and good wine to drink.
Speaks of the unknown and unseen God.

We all can know God and his Holy Spirit.
Through the love we see each day.
Through acceptance and forgiveness to those we meet.
We can open their eyes to the miracle of life.

The ultimate test in our lives today.
Is to reach out our hand to the lonely and sad.
To share with them the truth of life.
That's all LIFES CHALLENGES.

Which Way

I sat alone and watched the sea
Whirling and bashing against the quay
Doing the same both night and day.
It reminded me of a choice I made.

The sea has no choice which way to go
But in the bible God began to show
Good and bad seed people can sow
And it's sometimes difficult to know

Which way will you chose my friend today
Will you follow the easy or narrow way?
Follow the example God has shown
And ask the Lord His spirit to send

Will you give him your hand today?
Will you trust and follow his word
And let him guide you all the way
And speak the words that he would have you say

SECTION 3

Seeking and drawing

This is section is written at a time of seeking the Lord and of him drawing me
To his side and shows some of the many conversations I had with God
before I made my decision to follow Him

Back Into My Life

If only I'd let you back into my life
If only I'd let go of my pride
Your love would embrace me
Like the wings of a dove
And you'd lift me high on your love
Bring me again that joy and peace
If only I'd let you back into my life

So many fears that aren't from you
Pride and fear oh why my Lord
Why am I so wrapped up in myself?
Why am I so blind and cant feel your love?
Lord help me to love you, help me to see
You are the light at the end of the road
Oh lift me father in your heavenly love
And lead me to the cross and to life

When You Feel You Can't Go On

When you feel you can't go on
Just look to Jesus and the cross
He will give you all you need
To follow the straight and narrow way

Look to the cross where he died for you
Look to his head, his hands his feet
Feel the love that's in his heart
And you will never fear or fall

When things get too much in this world
Then rest in my arms and trust in me
Receive my peace, receive my strength
For I have power to overcome all

Sing his praise and worship him
Lift him high above the world
Then your spirit will rise before him
And he will touch and heal our lives

Turn Again My Precious Child

Turn again my precious child
and see the love in my eyes
Turn again my precious child
and see my arms open wide

Turn over to me all your pain
And I will heal and comfort you.
Turn over to me all resentment and fear
And I will make your heart renewed

Return to me your first love
And feel my love and peace
Return to me your first love
And feel all your pain released

Learn to trust in me again
Learn to call upon my name
Learn to walk my narrow way
And speak the words I say

The Ever Near Friend

Jesus is a friend who will always be there
If you trust and follow his way
If you will listen to all he will say
Then he will bring you, to a glorious day

When you feel like quitting and it's all up hill
Just rest in Jesus, in his presence be still
Till your strength from him returns
And once again Gods fire burns

Just ask for his wisdom and you will see
How you can set the captives free
The right words to say the actions to do
For all God's promises will remain true

Behold I come like a light in the darkness
Giving my truth to all who will hear
Then one day I'll come and take you home
Then I shall make earth and heaven anew

Thoughts Of Jesus

When I'm afraid I look to my lord
Look into eyes so full of love.
Look and see his arms open wide.
I look upon his hands his feet.
His heart was broken freely for me
On that Calvary tree of shame
So when I'm afraid or feel alone.
I remember all he did for me.
Then at last his peace fills my heart
With true and lovely thoughts of him
He is so strong, loving and kind.
He made the rain and wind so strong.
What does a good man have to fear?
Savior King and my guide
Take my hand and lead me on

Rest

Rest in my loving Jesus arms
Rest in him he will make no demands
Feel his arms securely around you
Giving you strength and peace anew

See in his eyes a love that is true
Feel his cleansing, making you new
Grow into love and joy untold
And see his purpose for you unfold

He loves the young ones and the old
His love alone more precious than gold
So rest in his arms and feel the peace
That comes from a love that knows no bounds

Rest in his arms and always be safe
Rest in his arms and you will win the race
Rest in his arms, have a smile on your face
And feel the warmth of his heavenly place

Lift My Spirit

When I look down to the sadness inside
I feel so sorry little and low.
But when I look up to Jesus above.
My heart is lifted and I feel glad

He lifts my spirit up to his throne.
And one with his spirit I will soar
Then I look down on the world below.
And God fills me with compassion from himself

Then he draws me to his side.
Tells me he loves and cares for me.
Gives me hope and peace anew
Holds me in his arms so true

At The Foot Of The Cross

Here I lay at the foot of the cross.
Here I lay all my hopes and fears.
Here where you give your life for me
Here where you suffered pain and shame.

Here I lay in your loving arms.
Here I stop worrying about my fears.
Here I give my whole self to you.
No fears, no doubts just pure, deep love.

Your love Lord Jesus is all I need.
All I need to keep me true.
You gave your life so freely for me
because you've loved me eternally

Take my worries far away
Fill me with your love today
I will love you forever more.
And only you I will adore

Lord give me strength each day I pray.
To keep me on the narrow way.
I need you always by my side.
To be my Savior and my guide.

I need your hand to see me through.
I need your word to see the truth
Lord put your hand in mine today
And keep me on the narrow way

Father Please Take Me

Father please take me into your arms.
And show me the way to go.
Break all the stubbornness in my mind
and in me an obedient servant find.
Take all the blocks that are in my mind.
Instead give me peace and joy combined
so I will find your perfect will.
And always for Jesus I will shine.

So every day and every night.
Help me Lord Take up the fight.
To set my life on wings of flight.
Shelter me always from evils sight

Help every battle for you to win
until in heaven your praises I will sing.
Oh what a wondrous glorious scene
To look back and see how far we have been

SECTION 4

Heaven and earth respond

This section represents some of the many conversations that
God and I had where I finally responded to
Gods calling and became his precious child

The Open Door

When you open the door, then you open your heart.
To an everlasting friend, who will never depart?
He will heal your hearts, and memories past.
And give you his strength to make it last.

When you reach out, your hand, and trust.
Then all your past life, will turn into dust.
Your life he will mold, just like the clay.
And bring you safe, into a sheltered bay.

If you will follow, and trust his way.
And never doubt the words he would say.
He'll be with you, come what may.
And bring your spirit, to eternal day.

Will you learn, to be his child?
Feel his love gentle and mild.
Draw from his strength each weary mile.
And bring to this world his eternal smile.

Sinner Come Back

Oh what joy, praise his name
A sinner strayed come back again.
Open the gates, shout from the walls
A weary soul's come home to rest
He's made the choice as he knows best.
Humbled himself, come back to God.
He's turned his back on sin and fear.
Asked the Lord forever to be near
Prepare the feast in the heavens above
A battle won through grace and love

Submit To Jesus

Jesus my Lord and my King.
Hear my heart as I sing.
Show me again your perfect will.
And you and I at last can be one.
And all of life's battles overcome
So dear Jesus as I sing
Reveal your fathers heart to me.
So I can safely see your way
and when the night has finally gone.
I can find my peace in knowing.
That Jesus is totally Lord of my life.
So father come and tell this child
wanting to know which way to go
give you the glory that's rightfully yours

Thoughts Of Jesus

When I'm afraid I look to my lord
Look into eyes so full of love.
Look and see his arms open wide.
I look upon his hands his feet.
His heart was broken freely for me
on that Calvary tree of shame
so when I'm afraid or feel alone.
I remember all the things he did for me.
Then at last his peace fills my heart
with true and lovely thoughts of him
He is so strong, loving and kind.
He made the rain and wind so strong.
What does a good man have to fear?
Savior King and my guide
Take my hand and lead me on

Kneel Before The Throne

I kneel before the throne of grace
Worship and praise you mighty king
Glorify and honor your holy name
Bow down and worship the prince of peace

Your throne is eternal you reign on high
Your mighty right hand guides and leads
My heart is in awe of your mighty power
And heaven is filled with your glorious light

Mighty councilor and risen Lord
Sword of the sprit truth and light
You fill my heart to overflow
With your mercy grace and love

All power is in you, my Lord and king
You hold the keys to life and death
You rule this earth with a mighty hand
Yet you know feeble frame and mind

Lord I am filled with mighty awe
As I stand before the throne of grace
I worship with angels singing your praise
My spirit is free and praise flows eternal

Look At The Good

When I'm as lonely as I can be
I can rejoice in the good that I see
The birds that sing up in the trees
The crisp autumn leaves in the breeze

I look into Gods eyes and see his love
Open my heart and hear his voice
Then he descends just like the dove
And lifts my heart to the mountains above

Sometimes we fail and wander away
Full of doubt, fear and pain
That's when my Lord to me will say
My child I forgive you again

I'll always forgive you, I'll always care
With me all your problems you can share
So turn from this world if you dare
And when you do I'll always be there

A Resonse From The Lord

I praise you Great and Mighty King.
I lift my hands to praise.
And worship, kneel at your feet.
All glory and honor belongs to you.
Your grace and mercy are beyond compare.

Come before my throne of grace.
Rest for a while no rushing away.
Learn from me and you will be free.
To live the life I want you to lead.

Unfold your arms so tightly around you.
Release your true praise to me.
Let go of rejection, its not who I am.
I died and gave my life to you.

You're accepted, you're forgiven.
Come and let me hold you ever near.
Take my hand and follow my lead.
Trust me to fill your every need.

Trust Me

All you need to do is trust me
All you need to do is share
All of your worries all of your cares
And leave the rest to me

I know the plans I have for you
And I will lead you there
You may not know what lies in store
But I love you so much you can be sure

Through all the noise and all the fear
You can come near and find your peace
For only I can fill the gap
That so many people feel today

So when you're afraid in pastures new
Just knock on the door and I'll open for you
I will show you great and mighty things
That you have never known

A Woman Sits Alone And Crys

A woman sits alone and cries.
At a table, empty and wide.
Remembers a time, laughter and talk.
Were the things to make her spirit sing?

Remembers those things, we will never know.
The first smile, the first kiss.
The word of love, so long ago.
The precious son, she held so close.

Now she sits and cries alone.
And often asks the reason why.
Why did you give him, and then take him away.
For a world full of sin and woe.

But as she walks to the sad tomb
She meets an angel with neat surprise.
Mary! Don't fear he is alive.

Now there's rejoicing, in her heart.
Now she knows the reason why.
Jesus died to set them free.
And gave his spirit eternally.

Gentle Spirit, Gentle God

Gentle spirit, gentle God
Come and speak, touch and heal
Speak with your voice of love and peace
Through your word and spirit wind

Touch our hearts oh father God
Touch our mind, body and soul
Through you precious holy spirit
Bring us deeper into you

Heal our loves and wounds so deep
Let us feel your love and peace
Heal our thoughts and attitudes
And help us live for you alone

SECTION 5

Challenging others

Having given my life to the Lord I found out how important it was to share our faith with others so they to have a chance to know and serve him

The Price Has Been Paid

One morning close to dawn I lay in my cell.
Alone and in fear my heart gave a yell
Is no one my friend is no one there.
Tomorrow I die and nobody cares

Then out of the darkness there came a light
A jailer with a lantern bringing me sight.
"Arise young man he said to me
The price has been paid and now you are free"

I got to my feet but just couldn't move
Just stood there alone shaking my head
I don't understand , this cannot be true
No one can give me my life anew

He said not a word just flung wide the door
You are free to go I cannot say more
I followed the jailer but still was not sure
If this was a trick wondered what was in store

My fear began to cease as the door came near
and I walked out my prison for the first time in years
But still how I doubted, could not believe
There was someone out there who cared for me

I looked through a gate and there stood a man
who looked into my eyes and held out his hand
Come my dear child and let me embrace you
With my love and forgiveness my love and my joy

Who are you I said with knee all aquiver
That you should want me my from to deliver
Then deep from my heart came the answer I sought
You are the man healing and deliverance taught

My child at last, the truth you see
I gave you my life when I died on the tree.
I'VE always been there, waiting patient and true.
For you to call me so I can heal you

"I could not save you till you called to me
Open the door of your heart and believe
I gave my life to set you free
from all of your sin pain and misery"

I fell to my knees and gave him my life
And begged him to teach me make me his child
He put out his hand and took my pain
And filled me with joy with his heavenly smile

He took my hand and led me away
Away from the prison and into new life
Away from the darkness and into the light
Never to fear the evils of night

So this is the story I promised to tell
Of an unseen friend who made me see
He will open the door if you give him the key
And all of your life you can walk free

So what will you do now my story is told
Ask Jesus your friend for strength to be bold
Ask Jesus your new life begin to mould
And reach that glorious much sought goal

When Churches Come Together

When churches come together
To do the will of God
Then I will send my spirit
With great and mighty power

When my spirit moves across the land
Then my peoples live will be changed
I will come and bless my people
And bring them close to me

When my people turn to praise me
Worship me in spirit and truth
Then I will speak my wisdom to them
And lead them on my narrow path

When they follow my will and trust in me
Then the world will see the truth
When the churches truly come one
Then they will be truly the family of God

Gods Workers Are Few

The harvest is ready, but the workers are few
More precious then flowers when kissed by the dew
So many are the people that don't know you
"If only" we say "what shall we do"

"What you shall do" the Lord said to me
"Go into this world and follow my lead"
"I will show you the ones to heal"
"I will show you the hungry to feed"

"Lord can it be me that will go for you"
"And give through you, people's lives anew"
"I am so weak I must tell you true"
"But still lord Jesus I will trust in you"

"At last my harvest is beginning to grow"
"And truly my people are beginning to know"
"That they are the people who will reap what I sow"
"And to hurting people my love would show"

So lets all be workers for the Lord today
Let us each one in our lives truly show
The knowledge of you that they need to know
And as we reap they too will sow

We all are important and precious to Him
If we allow him to forgive us our sin
Then work all our lives to make us whole
To send us out into this needy world

The Man By The Sea

There was a man, who lived by the sea.
Who came to die for you and me?
He came to set the captives free.
To bare our sins upon a tree.

He walked the earth to show the way.
And how we should live each day.
Open your hearts and hear him say
I'll be with you come what may.

He healed the sick, he raised the dead.
He even five thousand people fed
He made the pharos see red.
And filled every demon with fearful dread.

If you will love and trust his name.
And put your life in his picture frame.
Then today peace and life he will give,
And one day in heaven meet face to face.

Look To The Cross

Look to the cross and see Jesus saving.
Many a life and taking our sins.
He's taking our pain and making them his.
And through his wounds we are free to live.

Jesus lead me precious savior.
To the cross and make me see.
The price you paid upon that tree.
Has paid my debt indeed.

Lead me through the painful thorns.
Lead me through the flower fields.
Till at last your beauty I see.
And the golden crown upon your head.

Precious Jesus lead me on.
All my life till I meet with you.
Face to face with my dear savior.
Lead me to the promise land.

Christ And The Accuser

Once I dreamt upon a room.
With me and Satan and GOD
I stood before an alter bare
And Satan started to glare.

I am Satan the accuser, the father of all lies.
You stand condemned before me for all your sinful past.
You've listened to my thoughts and lies
You've gone the way I've told you too
So now its time to die

I am God her Lord and Savior
And there stands my precious child
I'VE loved her and lead her and now she is mine
So now it is time for her to live.

In a flash of light and a trumpet call
Gods son appeared on the alter bare
I saw the wounds of sacrifice
And I knew I'd been redeemed.

There lies before you my precious child
Who I sent to set my children free
Her sin and shame is washed away
I gave her my son now she is truly free

Satan couldn't stand before the truth
So he left with nothing to say
My father embraced me and gave me his peace
And lead me back to my room

That night I slept such a peaceful sleep
And when I woke in the morning light
I knew his love I knew his peace.
And laid my life down at his feet

The father loved us with a love so strong
That Jesus died a sacrifice for me
He gave his life so freely for us
Now what can we do for him

He is Christ the over comer and in him we can live
Through trials and pressure joys and woes
And spend an eternity praising him

Does Anyone Know

Does any one know about my lord?
Does any one know what pain he endured?
On that awful Calvary
Does any one know why he died for me?

He died because he loved us so.
He died to set us free from sin.
He gave up his glory in heaven above
To come to this sinful world below.

But now he has risen from the dead
And the church now has him at the head
He still would heal the sick the blind
If we would only trust in him

Trust in his redeeming blood.
Take his body and his love.
Take his precious holy spirit
Into our hearts and become one.

One in body one in mind
One in truth and love and joy
And when before his throne we stand
We will take this Promised Land

SECTION 6

⁓

Blessings and gifts

This section was written to rejoice in the good things that
Come through a relationship with God he wants to lead us and teach us
Pour his blessings on our lives

Power Of The King

I have felt the power of the king of all kings
When I have kneeled there at his feet
I have heard him saying, your life is now in me
And I will guide you to the end

I have felt the love of Jesus
When I took him into my heart
When He took my hand and said to me
My child just trust and walk with me

I have felt the grace of Jesus
As he forgave me from my sins
As he buried them in the deepest sea
At last I knew I was truly free

I have felt the compassion of Jesus
As I gave him my pain and hurts
My past life has died there on the cross
And all my life I now can be free

Have you felt his compassion, love and grace?
Have you kneeled before him in hope and faith?
Have you learned to trust him for every need?
You need only to trust and truly believe

He Is My Lord

He is my Lord, He is my king.
He is mine in everything
He holds my hand both night and day
and keeps me on the narrow way.

He leads me on from day to day.
Only with Jesus forever I will stay
when I feel weak He makes me strong
When I feel sad He makes me glad

Your Throne Of Grace

Lord I come before the throne of grace
I lift my hands and exalt your name
You reign supreme through all the world
Even kings and queens must bow the knee

Lord I come to your throne of grace
And gladly I will bow the knee
Put you upon the throne in my life
And live to worship and honor you

I will call upon you in my time of need
And you my lord will hear each word
You fill my life with spirit and righteousness
Lord let me live and shine for thee

Let my life shine with your glory
Let the fruits of your spirit be seen
Fill me today with your mighty power
And new hope for every day and night

You sit enthroned in majesty
You shine brighter than the mid day sun
One day we will see you face to face
Oh that great and glorious day

When you come back, up in the clouds
And take us home to thee
Then all your children will bow the knee
And praise you alone for eternity

There in the city, the city of gold
We will worship and sing your praise
Serve the mighty and glorious king
Live together in joy and peace

Trust For The Future

I cannot see the future
But all I have to do is trust
My savior Jesus sees it all
And he will guide me through

I do not know its twists and turns,
Its mountains, valleys and hills.
But I can trust my Jesus
And He will carry me through

I do not know its joys and pain
And every emotional high and low
But I know who holds my future
It's Jesus Christ my Lord

So today in faith I will take his hand
And let Him lead me on
Through all the joys and all the sorrow
Until he leads me home

Prophetic Poem

The harvest is coming beyond the horizon
My light is shining through the dark world
Have faith my children the time is drawing near
Behold look to the sky and see the signs
I will come with my heavenly angels
Coming to bring all my children home
So stretch fourth your hands to the coming king
Reach out your hand to the lonely and lost
My fire will come and purge your hearts
And make you pure in my sight
Make ready for the wedding feast
For I am coming soon
I'm preparing my church to be my bride
I'm coming with power and majesty
Release to me your heart felt praise
Lift your mind and spirit to me
Release your fears release you guilt
Come and make ready for your king

Kneel Before The Throne

I kneel before the throne of grace
Worship and praise you mighty king
Glorify and honor your holy name
Bow down and worship the prince of peace

Your throne is eternal you reign on high
Your mighty right hand guides and leads
My heart is in awe of your mighty power
And heaven is filled with your glorious light

Mighty councilor and risen Lord
sword of the sprit truth and light
You fill my heart to overflow
With your mercy grace and love

All power is in you, my Lord and king
You hold the keys to life and death
You will this earth with a mighty hand
Yet you know feeble frame and mind

Lord I am filled with mighty awe
As I stand before the throne of grace
I worship with angels singing your praise
My spirit is free and praise flows eternal

SECTION 7

A walk of faith

This section is written as I moved on through into Jesus
It's about my faith being built up and growing daily as
I trusted in God more and more

In The Stillness Of The Morning

In the stillness of the morning.
Let your voice alone be heard.
In the falling of the steady rain.
And the singing of the cheerful birds.

When the world has come to life.
With all its worries and strife.
Let us still have open ears.
To hear you're voice again oh Lord.

In the bustle of the afternoon.
Rushing to get the chores done.
Let's not forget to give God praise.
For leading us through another day.

In the quietness of the evening.
When we look back on our day.
Let us see your love shine through.
In all we've said and done.

In the darkness of the night.
When the world has gone to bed.
Thank the Lord who watches over us.
Who never sleeps but gives us rest.

Be Encouraged.

I will strengthen you
I will heal you
Give me your thoughts
give me your fears
I will set you free at last
From all that holds you back

Trust in me with all your heart
And you will see
how to stand upon my word
how to stand upon my truth

Stand in the mighty power of God
Stand in his grace and love
for you indeed are my precious child
and you have no need to fear

Set before you my word each day
Follow always in my way
Do what I say and say each word
and you will come to the victory

By His Stripes I Am Healed

By His stripes I am healed
By His blood I am washed
I am a new creation
And forever I am free

Wash me in your spirit
Purge me from my sin
Take away the shame I feel.
And bring me into peace

Cleanse me from all
Thoughts and attitudes
Cleanse my body, make me whole
Fill me with your power

Make me the child
Who is willing to be led
Let me eat of the word
And truly well be fed

Let your healing flow through me
And touch another heart
Show your loving grace through me
And let them truly see

You are the son who sets them free
When in faith they bend the knee
You have come to give them life.
And give them all eternity

Give Me A Servant Heart

Give me a servant heart Oh Lord.
One that will serve, and trust in you.
One that will follow, where you lead.
One that will obey every written word.

A heart that will always, put you first.
A heart that goes out, to the lonely and cold.
A heart that is filled, with goodness oh Lord.
A heart that is open, to all those in need.

Humble my heart, and change it today.
Keep me always, on the narrow way.
Help me to hear, what you want me to say.
To help lead a sinner, from night into day

Fill my heart, with love from you.
Fill my life, with grace and peace.
Fill my mind, with thoughts of you.
Fill my mouth, with praise anew.

Lord take my life, and come in anew.
Start in me a new work I pray.
Teach me and lead me, which way to go.
Until one day in glory I see.
The father that lovingly molded this child.

Honor The Lord

When you honor the Lord with body and soul
Then all else will melt in the sight of his praise
Empty ambitions and earthly desires
Will fade into pale in the light of his love

When we confess to our father above
All our sins both present and past
He will throw them into the deepest sea
Then he will say I remember no more

When you learn to trust the Holy Spirit
And put your faith in God alone
Then the spirit will lead and change you inside
And use you to tell others of his wonderful love

So Lord take my life and lead me on
Out into a world that needs you so much
Guide my words, my thoughts my deeds
Then take me home to the heavenly place

Jesus My Lord

Jesus my lord you're so precious to me
Jesus my lord you're so good to me
You keep me safe both night and day
And keep me in your precious way

I love you though you first loved me
So much so you died for me
There was no way but Calvary
To set this captive free

You laid your life down at the cross
And laid aside your majesty
What can I give to you my king?
I will give you my everything

Go In Faith

Go in faith and walk with me
Every step through out the day
I'll be your peace
I'll be your guide
On every step of the way

It may be hard
It may be good
You may see the darkness
But I am your light

I will shine a way for you
When in the dark valley you walk
So take my hand and walk by faith
And I will lead you all the way

To the end of the path
To that glorious day
Where I will see you face to face
And hold you in my arms

With My Spirit

With my spirit I will guide you
By my heart I will draw you into life
With my mind you will know my grace and truth
With my body broken you will have new life
With my hands I have sealed you forever
With my feet I leave footsteps where I carry you
With my grace comes new hope
With my love comes acceptance
With my Peace comes my rest
With my joy comes courage and strength
With my word comes all things revealed
Sink my words into your heart
Seek me in all that you do
Thrust that I will do the things that I say
And commit your life to me alone

❧ THE END ❧

Lightning Source UK Ltd.
Milton Keynes UK
UKOW04f0153030315

247158UK00001B/99/P